Cake Decorating

CONTENTS

This edition printed 1989 by
New Burlington Books
6 Blundell Street, London N7 9BH

Copyright © 1985 Quarto Publishing Limited.
First published in Great Britain in 1985

ISBN 1-85348-146-7

Printed by Leefung-Asco Printers Ltd,
Hong Kong

SIMPLE DECORATING TECHNIQUES

This section demonstrates the classic decoration of sponge cakes with soft fillings and coatings, including very easy designs with a dusting of icing sugar and more elaborate piped buttercream coverings. If you are a beginner, you will find here an introduction to some of the basic techniques and tools of cake decoration.

The techniques are simple but create attractive effects, and include diamond marking, cobweb icing and feather icing, grooving, swirling and peaking, two ways to decorate a Swiss roll and coating sponge with soft fondant icing. All the cakes are ideal for afternoon tea or even to celebrate an informal festive occasion.

Following these demonstrations will give you practice in using some of the basic tools of the trade — the turntable, palette knives, cake combs, piping bags and food colour — and at the same time help you develop your skills.

EQUIPMENT AND DECORATIONS

The techniques covered in this section require only fairly basic cake decorating equipment. The turntable is the most expensive item illustrated here, but if you are planning to take up cake decorating, it is worth having from the very beginning.

1 *A heavy-duty metal turntable. Cheaper models are available in plastic.*
2 *Food paste colours*
3 *Crystallized violets*
4 *Crystallized rose petals*
5 *Angelica*
6 *Glacé cherries*
7 *Piped sugar flowers*
8 *Real chocolate strands or vermicelli*
9 *Silver and coloured balls or dragees*
10 *Piping bag stand, with two filled piping bags and nozzles*
11 *Thick paintbrushes, for cleaning up around a partially finished cake*
12 *30 cm/12 in spatula*
13 *10 cm/4 in spatula or palette knife*
14 *Stainless steel rolling pin*
15 *Stainless steel profiled-edge scraper, for special effects on the side of a cake*
16 *Plastic scraper, for 'combing' the side of a cake*
17 *Parchment piping bag triangles*

DECORATING SPONGES

FILLING

A Victoria sandwich is traditionally filled with whipped cream and jam, either strawberry or raspberry, for a good contrast.

Spread one half of the cake with cream, and the other with jam, using a flat palette knife. Do not try to spread them one on top of the other. Sandwich the two halves together.

DUSTING

1 For a very pretty dusting on top of the cake, cover it with a paper doily and gently tap icing sugar from a sieve on to the cake.

2 Remove the doily very carefully or you will spoil the pattern beneath. Use this technique, too, with home-made stencils. If you are giving the cake as a present for example, you can stencil the person's name over the top.

COATING THE SIDES OF THE CAKE

Buttercream makes a very good coating for the sides of a sponge cake. It is particularly useful for a sandwich cake because it covers the join and gives a smooth finish. The cake can then be rolled in silver balls, chocolate nonpareils, chopped nuts, muesli or finely chopped glacé fruit.

1 Smooth the buttercream round the sides of the cake with a palette knife or smoother.

2 Fill your palm with chopped nuts or golden praline and brush the nuts against the buttercream all round the base of the cake.

3 If you want to coat the sides of the cake completely, spread a layer of the decoration (here, chocolate vermicelli) on a sheet of greaseproof paper and roll the cake in it, holding it flat between your palms.

GLACE ICING

Glacé icing can be coloured and flavoured. If you use a flavouring that is slightly coloured, use a colouring as well, or the result may be an unattractive off-white. Lemon juice heightens the whiteness of glacé icing. Orange flower water, peppermint oil and rose water are flavourings which will not discolour glacé icing.

1 To coat the top of the cake with glacé icing, carefully pour the icing out of the bowl, keeping up a steady stream. Stop as it ripples out to the edge, and smooth it if necessary with a dry palette knife. Tap the cake on the work surface to flatten and settle the icing.

2 If you want to decorate glacé icing, have your decoration at hand, because it sets quickly. Put the cake on its display plate straight away — the icing may craze if the cake is moved after it has dried.

TIP

Remember if the top of the cake is not perfect, you can turn it upside down and use the flat base for the top.

The cake OPPOSITE features chocolate vermicelli around the base, a piped rope of Bavarian buttercream around the edge, and segments of crystallized orange on the top. Simple decorations such as these can make something special out of the plainest cake.

ROSETTES

The sides and top of this cake have been decorated with buttercream, combed with a serrated comb, and a strip of golden praline laid around the base. The spiral effect on the top has been made by putting the cake on a turntable and holding a palette knife over it like the arm of a record player while the cake is rotated.

1 To make rosettes, fill a large piping bag with buttercream and use a star nozzle. Pipe the rosettes in a circular motion, one at a time — if you try to pipe them continuously, they will turn into scrolls.

2 Finish decorating the cake with green glacé cherries, cut into segments and positioned on the sides between the rosettes. Make a flower shape of glacé pineapple with a yellow glacé cherry for its centre on the top.

PEAKING

1 Cover the top of the sponge with butter icing and use a palette knife to pull it up into peaks.

2 Sprinkle the top with coloured strands and add a gold ribbon for a festive effect.

DIAMOND MARKING

1 Cover the sides of the sponge with chocolate vermicelli and spread the top with chocolate buttercream. Make a diamond pattern by pulling a skewer through the buttercream as shown.

2 Pipe simple shells round the edge of the top of the cake using a star nozzle and chocolate buttercream.

Simple decorating techniques can produce attractive results — the cake RIGHT is decorated with a serrated comb and piped rosettes; the chocolate cake BELOW is diamond marked with a border of piped shells.

SWIRLING

1 You can use a cake comb to create all sorts of patterns in butter icing. Hold the comb against the side of the cake as you rotate it on a turntable, or move it from left to right across the top to make waves, as here.

2 Pipe stars round the edge of the cake and finish it off with a white satin ribbon.

GROOVING

1 Use a cake comb with chocolate buttercream to create this complicated looking effect very simply. Rotate the cake on a turntable and move the comb sideways to make undulations. Be careful when you get back to the beginning of your pattern not to make a ridge. Use a deeply grooved comb on the sides of the cake.

2 Pipe a rosette in the centre, and beading around the top and bottom edges of the cake.

Always make a generous quantity of buttercream when decorating cakes like this one BELOW. A lot of buttercream is scraped off as the pattern is made.

COBWEB ICING

1 Pour the fondant over the top of the cake. Pipe concentric circles of chocolate icing, fondant or melted chocolate on the fondant. Start from the centre and work outwards. When the circles are completed, draw a skewer across the cake from the centre outwards, dividing it into quarters. Draw the skewer from the edge of the cake inwards, dividing it into eighths.

2 Hold the cake in the palms of your hands and roll the sides in green coloured coconut.

FEATHER ICING

Feathering is an attractive way of finishing off glacé icing or fondant. Fondant is used here. It takes slightly longer to set and gives you more time to work.

1 Pour the fondant over the top of the cake. The cake can have a marzipan base. Pipe straight lines of chocolate icing, fondant or melted chocolate across the cake. The best way of keeping the lines parallel is by working from the centre outwards. Starting at the centre of the cake, draw a skewer through the lines in the opposite direction, leaving a double

To colour coconut as for the cobweb-iced cake ABOVE, rub a little food colour on to your fingers and work them through the coconut. This method gives a good even colour.

space between the lines. Turn the cake round and repeat the process in the other direction creating a feather pattern.

2 Roll the sides of the cake in green coloured coconut and pipe a line of chocolate shells round the edge of the cake for a richer effect.

TRIANGULAR TOP

1 Spread one half of a Victoria sandwich with buttercream and pipe two rows of shells around the edge. Cut the second cake in half horizontally with a very sharp serrated knife. Dredge it with icing sugar, making a pattern through a doily. Cut it carefully into three. Position the three pieces on top of the cake with a cake slice. They will project like wings.

2 Pipe lines of cream shells over the joins. Decorate the top with split almonds, angelica and a cherry in the centre.

SPLIT TOP DECORATION

1 Spread one half of a Victoria sandwich with buttercream. Draw a line over the cream with a skewer to give the halfway mark. Pipe a double row of buttercream shells around half the cake, piping them more heavily in the middle than at the sides. Do the same around the other half if you want to create a butterfly effect with the finished cake.

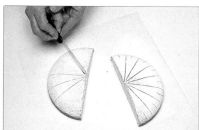

2 Use a very sharp serrated knife and carefully slice the second cake in half horizontally. Dredge the top with icing sugar and cut the cake in

half. Mark a decorative pattern in the icing sugar with a skewer as shown.

3 Being careful not to touch the top of the cake with your fingers, which would leave prints, place the two halves in position on top of the buttercream shells using a cake slice. One half should stand open resting on the buttercream shells or both if you have piped shells around both sides.

4 Pipe a line of buttercream shells across the join and decorate with cherries and angelica.

DECORATING ROLLS

Cylindrical cakes can either be made with sponge mixture and rolled up or with fruit mixture baked in a cylindrical tin.

SWISS ROLL

1 Cover the Swiss roll with buttercream, taking it down the sides. Leave the underside and the ends uncovered.

2 Dip the sides of the cake in chocolate vermicelli and either pipe ridges along the top with a fine tube or mark ridges with a fork.

3 Pipe a line of shells across the centre of the cake and decorate it with walnuts, cherries and angelica.

The ridges on this decorated Swiss roll BELOW can either be piped or marked with a small fork.

COATING A ROUND CAKE

Prepare the cake by glazing with warm apricot jam and/or coating with marzipan. Melt the fondant in a double boiler and add stock syrup to thin it down if necessary.

1 Stand the cake on a wire rack and pour the fondant carefully on to the centre of it. Give it a fairly thick coating so that it will run over the sides of the cake. The excess will drip through the mesh of the rack.

2 Use a palette knife to smooth over the top and sides of the cake. Tap the wire rack a few times on the work surface to settle the icing. As it settles, it will drip off the base. It is important to use a wire rack, so that the fondant does not build up at the bottom of the cake and spoil its shape.

COATING A SQUARE CAKE

1 Prepare the fondant as for a round cake, and stand the square cake on a wire rack. Pour the fondant over the cake from corner to corner in a diagonal cross.

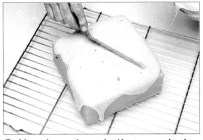

2 Use the palette knife to push the fondant from the centre of the cake to the sides and down the edges, working fairly fast before it starts to set. Tap the wire rack on the work surface to settle the fondant and dislodge any air bubbles.

PIPING WITH FONDANT

1 Add a little melted chocolate to some fairly runny fondant and pipe it straight from the piping bag, cut off at the point to give a fine line. Embroidery pattern books are a good source of ideas for attractive designs.

2 A more complicated design is piped on the round cake, using five colours of fondant. To stop the petals flowing into each other, pipe alternate petals and wait for them to set slightly before piping the petals in between.

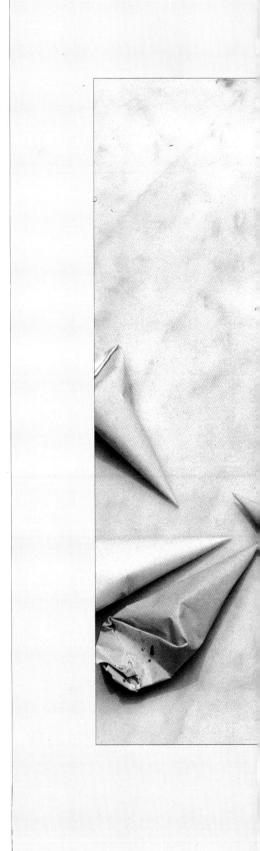

Fondant is piped straight from the bag without a nozzle. It can be used to create fairly intricate effects as shown RIGHT.

ELABORATE DECORATING TECHNIQUES

Before attempting one of the elaborate royal- or fondant-iced cakes make sure you are familiar with the techniques demonstrated in this section. A useful way of practising is to ice a polystyrene cake dummy and then try out the different piping techniques on it. This will help you choose your cake design, by giving you a chance to discover which types of decoration you like and find easy.

This section opens with the fundamentals — basic equipment and icing nozzles, covering with marzipan, royal and fondant icing, and making a piping bag. It then demonstrates a variety of piping techniques, making lace, run-outs, piping flowers and borders, and finally making templates for positioning pillars on tiered cakes and assembling tiers.

EQUIPMENT

The equipment illustrated opposite is a selection of items used in the decoration of elaborate royal- and fondant-iced celebration cakes.

1 Heavy-duty icing turntable
2 Plaster wedding cake pillars
3 Plastic wedding cake pillars, with hollow centres for wooden skewers
4 Polystyrene cake dummy for practising and display purposes
5 Wooden skewers
6 A selection of shaped 4cm/½ in thick cake boards and thin cake cards
7 Large flexible plastic icing smoother for fondant icing
8 Small stainless steel scraper for royal icing
9 Small flexible plastic smoother
10 Stainless steel straight edge for applying royal icing
11 Short spatula for general mixing and filling work
12 Handled smoother for fondant icing — an alternative to the large flexible smoother
13 Silver banding for cakes and cake boards

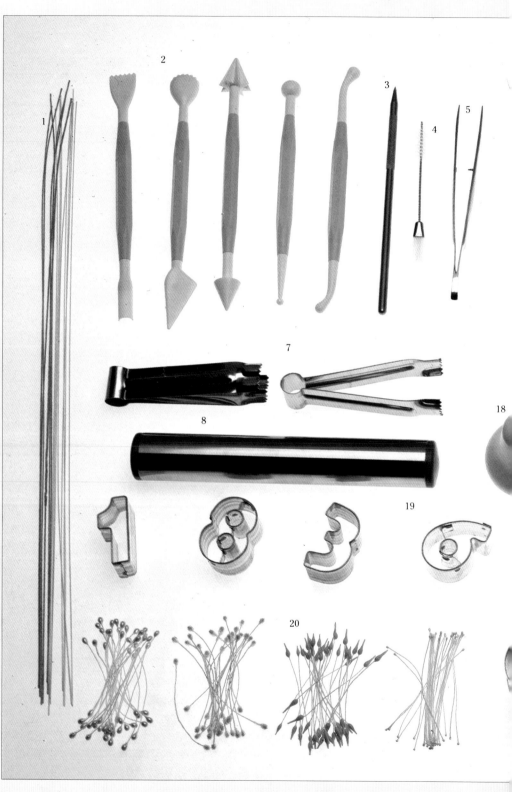

Illustrated here is a selection of tools used in elaborate cake decoration.

1 Cotton-coated floristry wire
2 Modelling tools (from left to right): paddle and U shape (No. 4); Shell and blade (No. 2); Cone and star tool (No. 5); Ball tool (No. 3); Dog bone shape (No. 1)
3 Stainless steel scriber, for marking patterns on to icing
4 Nozzle cleaning brush
5 Fine-pointed tweezers
6 Cranked handle palette knife
7 Set of crimpers
8 Stainless steel rolling pin
9 Selection of fine paintbrushes
10 Selection of edible food colour
11 Strong paste food colours
12 Dry colour
13 Frill or flounce cutter
14 Flower cutters (top row from left to right): Briar rose; Serrated rose leaf; Blossom-shaped plunger cutters; (bottom row) Star or rose calyx cutters; Rose petal or azalea petal cutters
15 Selection of 1cm/½ in aspic cutters
16 Flower nails
17 Selection of graduated biscuit cutters
18 Hollow plastic bell-shaped moulds
19 Selection of numeral cutters
20 Artificial stamens

ICING NOZZLES

There are many different kinds of icing nozzle on the market. It is better to buy the more expensive nozzles because they have very finely cut edges, which give accurate shapes and are more durable. If you buy inexpensive nozzles and find that the edges are rather rough or banned, file them down with emery paper.

All the shapes — star, shell, petal, basket weave, leaf and so on — come in varying widths. A full range comprises between 15 and 25 sizes.

To begin with you will need a fine writing nozzle, which is round and also produces a beaded 'snail trail', a shell nozzle and perhaps a petal nozzle. With these three basic tools you can create a wide range of designs.

Icing nozzles should always be kept clean — even a fine obstruction, such as a hair, can spoil the regular outline of the shape you are trying to pipe. A special icing nozzle brush is available for cleaning nozzles.

Different manufacturers use different numbers to designate the widths of the nozzles, but smaller numbers always refer to finer nozzles. The nozzles used in this book are made by Bekenal Products Ltd.

It is possible to pipe without a nozzle, straight from the bag (the leaves on the Valentine cake on p. 126 were made without nozzles and chocolate work is usually done without nozzles), but the addition of a few nozzles to your icing kit will give you greater scope and variety.

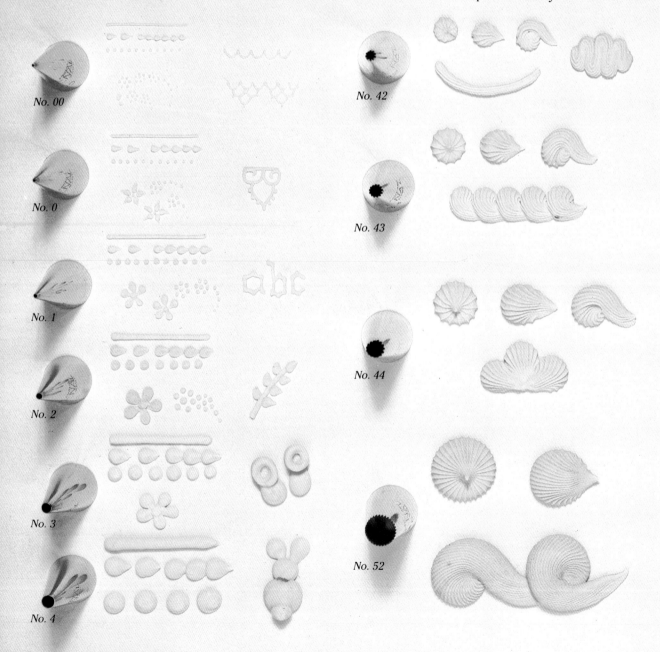

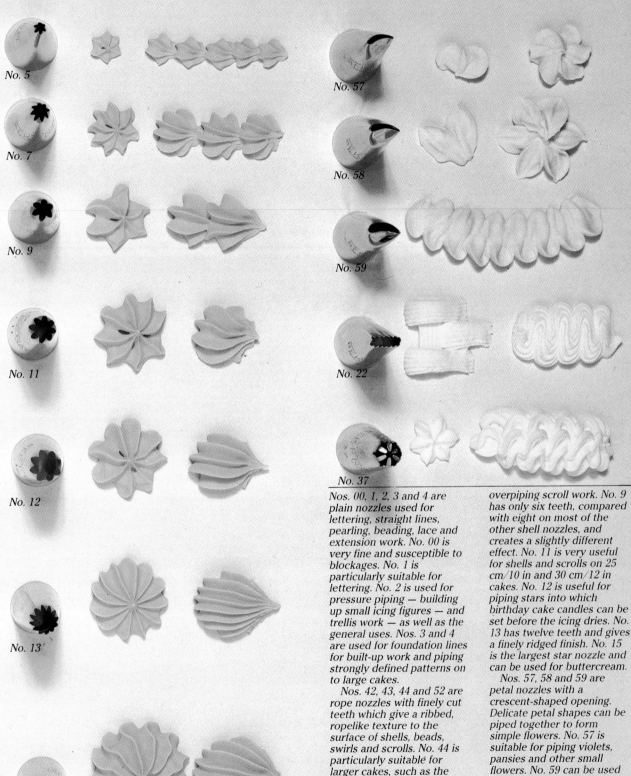

No. 5

No. 7

No. 9

No. 11

No. 12

No. 13

No. 15

No. 57

No. 58

No. 59

No. 22

No. 37

Nos. 00, 1, 2, 3 and 4 are plain nozzles used for lettering, straight lines, pearling, beading, lace and extension work. No. 00 is very fine and susceptible to blockages. No. 1 is particularly suitable for lettering. No. 2 is used for pressure piping — building up small icing figures — and trellis work — as well as the general uses. Nos. 3 and 4 are used for foundation lines for built-up work and piping strongly defined patterns on to large cakes.

Nos. 42, 43, 44 and 52 are rope nozzles with finely cut teeth which give a ribbed, ropelike texture to the surface of shells, beads, swirls and scrolls. No. 44 is particularly suitable for larger cakes, such as the lower tiers of a wedding cake. No. 52 is used for very large scrolls and curves. This nozzle requires a larger piping bag.

Nos. 5, 7, 9, 11, 12, 13 and 15 are shell or star nozzles. No. 5 is mainly used for piping shell borders around the base of cakes and for

overpiping scroll work. No. 9 has only six teeth, compared with eight on most of the other shell nozzles, and creates a slightly different effect. No. 11 is very useful for shells and scrolls on 25 cm/10 in and 30 cm/12 in cakes. No. 12 is useful for piping stars into which birthday cake candles can be set before the icing dries. No. 13 has twelve teeth and gives a finely ridged finish. No. 15 is the largest star nozzle and can be used for buttercream.

Nos. 57, 58 and 59 are petal nozzles with a crescent-shaped opening. Delicate petal shapes can be piped together to form simple flowers. No. 57 is suitable for piping violets, pansies and other small flowers. No. 59 can be used to create an attractive pleated ribbon effect.

No. 22 is used for piping a basket weave effect.

No. 37 can be used to make a simple flower with one squeeze of the piping bag, or a braided effect, by piping continuous, slightly uneven lines.

COVERING WITH ROYAL ICING

Leave the marzipan for two or three days for the surface to harden slightly before you ice the cake. If you are working in damp conditions, you may have to put the cake in an airing cupboard or a warm dry place.

Make up the royal icing with a sufficient quantity to give the cake three coats. Give the cake top a coat with the freshly made icing, which should be well aerated from beating. Always keep the bowl of icing covered as you work. Let the top dry for about six hours or overnight before you start to work on the sides. Do not try and hurry the drying process — if you dry it in a low oven the icing will discolour, and it may crack as the cake expands and contracts.

In this instance only, it does not matter if air bubbles are present, as the first layer of icing serves to provide a foundation on which subsequent finishing coats are applied.

1 Place the cake on a turntable. Put the equivalent of two or three tablespoons of icing in the centre of the cake with a palette knife. The blade of the knife should be about 20 cm/8 in long.

2 With a paddling motion, spread the icing towards the sides of the cake. Turn the cake as you tilt and rock the blade of the knife in the icing, being careful to even it out and eliminate any air bubbles.

3 Smooth round the cake in a fan pattern, turning the cake and drawing the knife out from the centre to the edges. Flatten the fan pattern in two or three sweeps, using the turntable and keeping the knife still.

4 Take a straight-edge or a ruler, longer than the diameter of the cake. Hold it at either end, tilt it at an angle to the cake and pull it smoothly across the surface, to the edge of the cake. Pivot the straight-edge so that its other long edge is in contact with the icing and push it gently away from you. You should have icing sticking only to one face of your straight-edge. Maintain an even and steady pressure with both hands as you move the straight-edge over the cake.

If after one sweep, you have not got a smooth surface, repeat the process.

If you still have not got a smooth top after three or four attempts remove as much icing as is practical, beat the mixture and start again from Step 2. Do not despair since the first coat need not be immaculate. It does not even matter if it is so thin that you can see the marzipan through it, as all you need to do is to create a smooth seal. The second coat will hide any minor flaws and give you a perfect base for the following coat.

5 When working on the sides of a cake use a stainless steel smoother to remove the excess icing. A plastic one might bend with the weight of the icing. Hold the smoother at an angle against the side of the cake and rotate the turntable. As the icing piles up on the smoother, scrape it off into the bowl of unused icing.

6 To cover the sides, take some icing on the palette knife and rock it backwards and forwards on the cake as you rotate the turntable. Keep the knife in the icing so that it is pushed forwards on to the marzipan to eliminate any air bubbles. Repeat the process until the sides are completely coated and have a reasonably smooth finish.

7 Smooth the sides of the cake in one continual sweep. Start with both hands on the furthest side of the cake, holding the smoother in one and the turntable in the other.

8 Rotate the turntable towards you so that your hands meet up at their starting point. When the circle is completed, pull the smoother off gently towards you.

9 Go round once more with the smoother to neaten the join between the sides and the top of the cake.

10 If you have not had time to allow the top to dry, omit Step 9, because you may spoil the clean edge. Allow the icing to dry and use a very sharp knife gently to carve away the rough edge of icing at the join. Apply the second and third coats in the same way.

11 To cover the cake board, put some icing on the board with your palette knife and turn the table, dragging the icing round it for about 10 cm/4 in. Repeat the process all around the board.

12 Use the smoother to finish off and stop the icing building up around the sides of the cake. Hold the smoother still and rotate the turntable with your other hand, smoothing all around the board in one sweep.

13 Hold the palette knife at an angle to the board and rotate the turntable to trim off any icing the smoother has pushed over the edge.

Rough icing is particularly suitable for Christmas cakes where the textured surface is used to resemble snow.

ROUGH ICING

If you are icing a cake for the first time and are unable to get the icing smooth, you can always turn it into rough icing. This method is also useful if you want to ice a cake in a hurry.

1 Put the royal icing on the cake as before and use a paddling motion with the palette knife to bring it out to the edges of the cake. Pull up peaks of icing all over the cake with the flat side of a knife.

2 Alternatively, use a slightly damp but not wet piece of foam rubber sponge. This will give a lighter, more delicate texture than the knife.

PIPING BAGS

For intricate decorating work, paper piping bags are essential. They are far superior to the metal variety, as they are so much more flexible to handle.

If you are doing multi-coloured work or using different nozzles, have several piping bags ready.

MAKING A PIPING BAG

Making paper piping bags for fine decorative work is not difficult. Use either greaseproof or waxed paper or use packs of ready-cut paper available from specialist sources.

1 Cut a 25cm/10in square of greaseproof or waxed paper. Fold it in half diagonally to make a triangle. Mark points (A), (B) and (C) in the corners as illustrated.

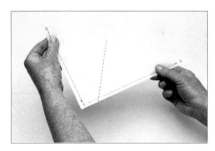

2 With the point of the triangle (C) facing towards you and holding the triangle at points (A) and (B), fold (B) round and back over (A).

3 Hold point (A) firmly and pull point (B) towards you to complete the cone shape. Take point (B) round to meet point (C).

4 To secure the piping bag, fold in the loose ends over the top edge and staple them together.

FILLING A PIPING BAG

1 Cut off the tip of the piping bag and insert the required nozzle.

2 Hold the piping bag in your left hand with your thumb at the back for support.

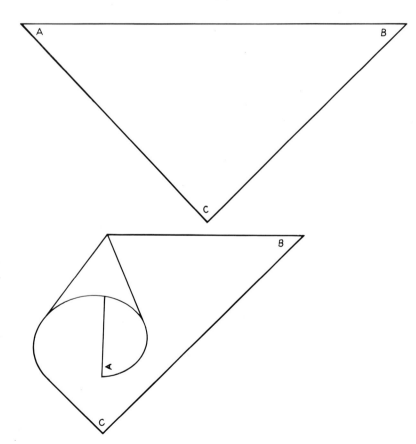

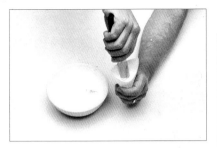

3 Using a palette knife, fill the bag half to two-thirds full. Push the icing down into the back of the bag against your thumb. Take care not to overfill as the icing may overflow from the top or the bag may burst.

4 With your thumb, push the back of the bag right down over the icing.

5 Carefully fold the sides of the bag in towards the centre, then fold over the top, pushing the icing down gently towards the tip. Fold over one corner again, making a pad to push with your thumb.

TIP

Have a damp cloth at hand to wipe the nozzle in between pipings and to help stop the tube getting clogged with hardened icing. If using several bags to decorate a cake, always cover the tips of them when not in use with a damp cloth, or stand them nozzle downwards in an icing bag stand filled with a dampened sponge.

HOLDING A PIPING BAG

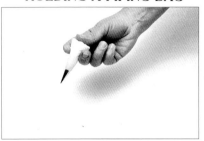

1 Hold the piping bag between your middle and index fingers and push with your thumb.

2 Place the tip of the nozzle in position over the work, before beginning to push the icing through the bag. Pressing down with your thumb on the folded part of the bag, squeeze out the icing. Pressing with and releasing your thumb will cause the icing to flow, then stop. Because the icing continues to flow after the pressure has stopped, you must release the pressure on the bag before you

reach the end of the line to be piped you watch carefully to see how tl icing flows, you will quickly learn judge the pressure and moveme required to produce even, we formed lines and shapes.

3 Once you have mastered piping straight lines, try using a star nozzle for shells. Position the nozzle on the surface where you want to pipe the shell. Without moving the bag, push out the icing. Once the shell has formed, pull the bag back to form a tail. Position the bag to form the next shell so that it just overlaps the tail of the first one.

PIPING TECHNIQUES

The consistency of the icing is the most important factor in piping. It should not be too stiff — it must be light and fluffy, and it must hold a peak.

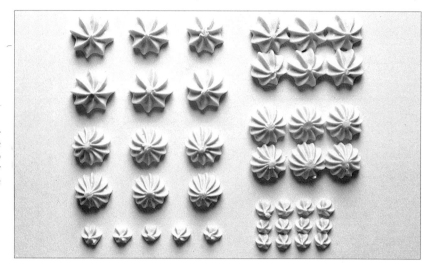

STARS

Hold the bag, fitted with the appropriate nozzle, perpendicular to the surface to be iced. Press on the bag to release the icing, then pull it up gently to form a point and a star shape will be formed.

ROSETTES

These rosettes are made with fine rope nozzles, which have shallower indentations than the star nozzles. With the bag held perpendicular to the surface to be iced, pipe a circle. Lift the nozzle slightly, apply pressure, bring it round to the centre and release the pressure as you tail it off.

SCROLLS

Pipe scrolls with fine rope nozzles, as for rosettes, but instead of tailing off into the circle, come out of it, creating a C- or an S-shape. For a C-shape, work in an anticlockwise motion. For an S-shape, take the nozzle round clockwise. You can make attractive patterns by combining the C and the S, and if you twist the nozzle as you pipe, you will get a rope effect.

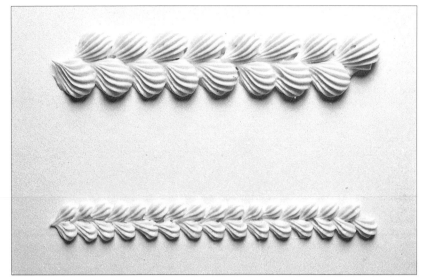

ALTERNATING SHELLS

Follow the instructions for shells, but take the point down at an angle of 45 degrees. Pipe a second row of shells beneath the first, taking the points up. Start with your piping nozzle at the tail of the upper shell for a plait effect.

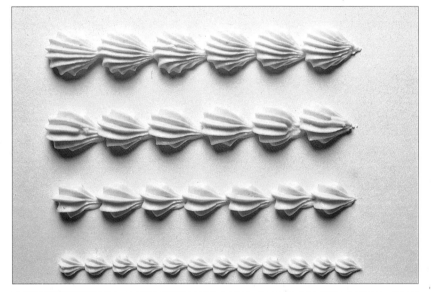

SHELLS

Rest the appropriate nozzle on the surface where you want to pipe the shell. Push out the icing without moving the bag. Once the shell has formed, pull the bag back to form a tail. Position the bag to form the next shell so that it just overlaps the tail of the one in front.

FLEUR DE LYS

This shape can be piped with a shell nozzle or fine rope nozzle, or you can even use a plain round nozzle for a smooth effect. First pipe a shell with a long tail. Then pipe an S-shape scroll to the left and a C-shape scroll to the right. You can pipe the flowers in the same way. Pipe one set of petals, and overpipe the second set.

STRAIGHT LINES

Touch the surface where you want to pipe. Lift the tube and apply pressure so that the icing flows out in a straight line. Drop it down at the other end of the line after you have released the pressure and the icing has stopped flowing. Do not attempt to pipe a straight line by dragging the nozzle along the surface of the cake or waxed paper. All you will succeed in doing is damaging the fine edge of the nozzle and indenting the surface of the cake. The nozzle must be lifted off the surface.

Overpiping is a classic piping technique. It is difficult and requires a very steady hand. By piping straight lines of varying widths touching each other, you can create a classic three-dimensional effect. Let each line dry before you begin on the next. If you are using this technique on a wedding cake, complete all your piping with one width nozzle before you change to the next. If you make a mistake, you can correct it with a slightly damp paintbrush, by pushing the line back into shape.

TRELLIS

Pipe one set of parallel lines, then overpipe a second either at right angles for squares, or with both sets of lines on the diagonal for diamonds. Use another width nozzle for overpiping to create a different effect.

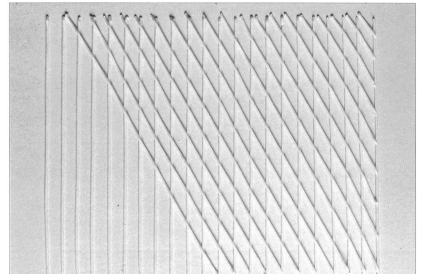

ZIGZAGS

These can be piped in a continuous line with any shaped nozzle. Until you are more confident, you may find it easier to stop and start at each point — this will give a very definite V-shape to the zigzag.

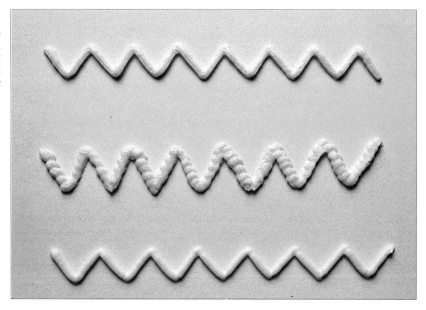

RAISED TRELLIS OR NETS

This is a style that was very popular a couple of decades ago. It has rather gone out of fashion because it is time-consuming. You can build up from the base with trellis work, but it is quicker and just as effective to pipe an oval scroll with a fine rope nozzle and cover it. Anchor the icing, twist the nozzle to form a rope as you apply the pressure, then release the pressure and taper off. Overpipe with a fine round nozzle, making parallel diagonal lines. Overpipe again in the opposite direction. You can build up the net by overpiping with decreasing sized nozzles in different directions.

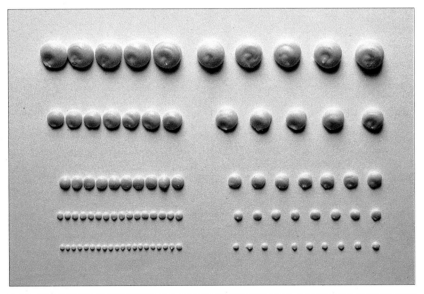

DOTS AND BEADS

The difficulty with piping dots and beads is disguising the take-off point, which will tend to make a tail. This is harder to disguise, the bigger the bead you are piping. Using constant pressure keep the point of the nozzle stationary in the bead until it is the size required. Release pressure on the bag after piping the bead and then take off gently to the side. Correct any mistakes with a slightly dampened brush once the bead is nearly dry by gently pressing any projecting point down into the mass of icing.

TWISTED ROPE

Twisted rope can be piped with a plain writing nozzle or a shell nozzle as well as a rope nozzle. The trick is to twist the bag as you are piping. Keep constant pressure on the bag. To avoid varying the width of the rope, hold the bag at an angle and rotate it as you go.

COVERING WITH MARZIPAN

FOR ROYAL ICING

A common problem with cakes covered in marzipan and then royal icing is that the icing becomes discoloured by the marzipan beneath. This happens usually because there is too much oil in the marzipan and it has not been allowed to dry thoroughly before being covered with icing. Allow the cake plenty of time to dry and use a cooked, not uncooked, marzipan.

This problem does not occur with bought marzipan. If possible, choose white or naturally coloured marzipan.

1 Always turn the cake over to decorate it, so that the flat base becomes the top. What is now the base of the cake may be concave or convex and this should be dealt with. Either slice off the rounded part if it is concave or fill the hollow with marzipan if it is convex.

2 Roll a long, thin sausage of marzipan and stick it round the base of the cake with jam or egg white by pressing it in to the cake with a palette knife. This will both seal the edges of the cake to the cake board and help the cake to keep longer.

3 Sprinkle the work surface with icing sugar. Roll out the marzipan, using spacers as a guide to even thickness and the right width, which should be a little more than the measurement across the top of the cake.

4 Turn the marzipan over, sprinkling more icing sugar beneath it if necessary. The smoother rolled side of the marzipan is the 'right' side. Brush a circle of warm apricot jam or egg white the same size as the diameter of the cake on the 'wrong' side of the marzipan. Alternatively, brush the cake with jam. Apricot is generally used rather than other jams because it does not dominate the flavour of the marzipan.

5 Place the cake top down on the marzipan. Cut the marzipan closely round the cake.

6 Turn the cake the right way up, being careful not to leave finger marks in the marzipan. Trim off any excess marzipan from the bottom sausage. Ensure that the sides of the cake are smooth, filling any small holes with pieces of marzipan.

7 Roll out a strip of marzipan about 5mm/¼in thick for the sides of the cake. The length of the strip should be three times the diameter of the cake. Measure the depth of the strip to fit the sides. Make sure your work surface is well dusted with icing sugar. Turn the marzipan over, so that the smoother side is face down. Brush the marzipan with warm apricot jam.

8 Roll the cake along the marzipan, pressing it into position. If you have miscalculated, and you need to add a little extra marzipan, it will not show if the joins are neat.

9 If you are covering a square cake, measure the sides of the cake and cut two pieces to fit. Attach them to opposite sides of the cake and measure the two remaining sides plus the thickness of the marzipan before cutting and fitting. This will give you 90-degree corners. Otherwise follow the instructions for the round cake.

10 Now the cake is completely covered, smooth it carefully with the heel and palm of your hands. A smooth, flat coating of marzipan will provide the perfect base for a professional coating for the cake.

FOR FONDANT ICING

If you intend to finish your cake with fondant rather than royal icing, a slightly different technique for putting on the marzipan is involved. The marzipan needs to be rounded at the corners and edges, because the fondant is applied to the top and sides of the cake in one process. Use warm apricot jam or egg white to hold the marzipan in position.

Fondant icing does not become discoloured by marzipan in the way that royal icing does, so either natural or coloured marzipan can be used.

1 Turn the cake upside down, so that the flatter surface becomes the top. Trim the sides if necessary and fill any holes with marzipan dampened with egg white. Roll a long, thin sausage of marzipan for the base of the cake, paint the edge of the cake with egg white and attach the marzipan.

2 Press the marzipan on to the cake with a palette knife to secure it. Do not use your fingers.

3 Turn the cake the right way up and place it on a sheet of greaseproof paper. Moisten the cake all over with egg white.

4 Roll out a square of marzipan large enough to cover the top and sides of the cake, allowing for some surplus.

5 Pick up the marzipan right-side up. Use your right hand to pick up the marzipan and slide it over your left hand. Drape it over the cake.

6 Hold the marzipan up from beneath with one hand and smooth it down with the other towards the raised hand to exclude air bubbles.

7 Once the top is flat, flare out the corners. Make sure you do not stretch the marzipan too much, or it will crack and craze. Smooth and fit the corners using the palm of your hand before you fit the sides. Make sure the sides are flat and not pleated or creased.

8 Use the warmth of your hand to help smooth off the marzipan and ensure it is well fixed to the cake.

9 With a palette knife trim the marzipan to the base of the cake making a neat edge all the way around.

MARZIPAN ANIMALS

Marzipan animals make delightful decorations for children's birthday cakes. The basic ideas demonstrated here can easily be adapted to other animals and figures.
You will need a variety of modelling tools and kitchen equipment.

RABBIT

1 Take a piece of white marzipan the size of an egg and roll out a cone for the rabbit's body. Make an indentation where the tail will fit. Make indentations at the larger end of the cone for the haunches. Roll a small ball of marzipan for the head.

2 Make an indentation with your little finger across the head, and roll it into a dumbell shape.

3 Cut down the length of the thinner end to form the ears, which you can line with pink marzipan if you wish.

4 Indent little holes for the eyes and nose. Fill in the eyes with white royal icing and add a cone of pink marzipan for the nose. Paint black dots for the eyeballs. Try to suggest that the rabbit is looking slightly to one side. With the 'U' tool, indent a smiling mouth.

5 Make a little carrot out of orange and green marzipan. Divide the pointed end of the cone to make the front legs, slightly open them out and fix the carrot between them. Fix the head on the body with egg white, royal icing or melted chocolate.

SCOTTIE DOG

1 Roll a sausage of dark brown marzipan about 10 cm/4 in long and 1.5 cm/³⁄₄ in thick. Cut off a quarter for the head and mark the remaining piece to divide it into three.

2 Snip a piece from the top of the rolled marzipan and lift it gently to form the tail. Cut through the sausage from beneath the tail to the end to form the back legs. The front legs are formed in same way.

3 Twist the legs apart gently and arch the marzipan to form the dog's body. Adjust the legs so that the dog stands firmly. Mark its paws.

4 Take the head and pinch up two ears with your thumb and forefinger. Indent the ears with the dog bone tool.

5 Pull out the dog's whiskers by stroking with the thumb and forefinger, and snip it into a fringe with the scissors.

6 Press a small ball of pink marzipan between the whiskers to form the mouth, and add a red tongue. Make a depression for the nose and insert a small cone of black marzipan.

7 Make two indentations for the eyes and fill them with white royal icing. Paint on black dots to complete the eyes.

8 Position the head on the body at an angle and fix it in place. The Tam'o'shanter cap is made by rolling red and green marzipan together and pressing a red pompom on top. Complete the model by giving the dog a bone.

GOLDFISH

1 Roll out a sausage of orange marzipan 2.5 cm/1 in thick and 7.5 cm/2½ in long. Make two indentations, one with the little finger very close to one end to form the mouth, and the second with the index finger a little further from the other end to form the goldfish's tail.

2 Stroke the marzipan between the thumb and forefinger to form a fin on the top of the fish, and press and flatten the other end to form the tail. Turn the tail slightly to one side so that the fish will stay upright.

3 Mark wavy lines on the fins and dent surface of body to form scales.

4 Make the side fins by moulding small cones of marzipan and flattening and curling them into shape. Fix them on the sides of the fish with egg white. Pipe royal icing for the eyes into the sockets. When the icing is dry, paint black dots to complete the eyes.

DUCK

1 Roll four balls of white marzipan, one 5 cm/2 in across for the body, one 4 cm/1½ in across for the head, and two 1 cm/½ in across for the wings. Roll two balls of orange marzipan, one 4 cm/1½ in across for the feet and one 5 mm/¼ in across for the beak. Form the large white ball into a cone and drag the tip end of the cone across the work surface to form the uptilted tail. Squeeze the medium-sized white ball gently.

2 Flatten the two smallest white balls into teardrop shapes for the wings. Mark in feathers from the shoulder to the tip. Feather-mark the tail in the same way. Elongate the larger orange ball for the feet by forming a depression across the centre.

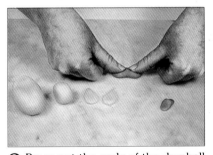

3 Press out the ends of the dumbell with your thumbs to make the feet. Roll the other ball into a cigar shape and fold in half to form the beak. Pinch the beak up in the middle so that it forms an open 'V' shape.

4 Assemble the duck. Fix the body on the feet with egg white or melted chocolate. Position the beak on the body of the duck and press the head on top, sandwiching the beak between the head and body. Attach the wings with egg white and pipe in the eyes with white royal icing. Mark the eyeballs and eyebrows. Add character with a little hat and by making a simple umbrella from a cone of marzipan and slipping it between a wing and the body.

FROG

1 Form a ball of green marzipan 5 cm/2 in across into a pear shape, and flatten and bend it over slightly at the top. Slice through the narrowest part with a sharp knife to form the mouth. Taking about half as much marzipan again, roll a dumbell shape with one end larger than the other (as with the rabbit above). Roll two smaller balls for the protruding eye sockets.

2 Cut the dumbell shape in half along its length to make the frog's legs. Twist the smaller end outwards to form the foot and mark the webbed feet.

3 Attach the legs and eye sockets to the body and make indentations for the eyeballs. Pipe in the eyeballs with white royal icing and complete the eyes with dots of black.

TEDDY BEAR'S PICNIC

This delightful cake makes an ideal centrepiece for a children's party. You can add more or less detail according to the time available.

INGREDIENTS
1 × 20 cm/8 in round rich fruit cake
warm apricot jam, mixed with a little
  water
350 g/12 oz marzipan
700 g/1½ lb fondant icing
450 g/1 lb gelatin icing
125 g/4 oz royal icing for fixing

MATERIALS & DECORATIONS
1 × 25 cm/10 in round cake board
cocktail stick
small pastry cutter
fine paintbrush
Food colours: blue, green, red, yellow,
  black, silver

1 Turn the cake upside down. Spread with warm apricot jam. Roll out the marzipan and cover the cake. Leave to dry for 12 hours.

2 Take 225 g/8 oz fondant icing. Moisten the marzipan on the cake. Roll the fondant out into a circle and mould it over the top and sides of the cake, cutting away any surplus. Leave to dry for several hours.

3 Take 125 g/4 oz gelatin icing and colour pale blue. Roll out the icing and cut out a 20 cm/8 in square to make the tablecloth. Leave to dry. Position the cloth on the cake and leave to dry.

4 Paint a rough check design on the tablecloth with different food colours. Paint flowers and grasses around the sides of the cake.

5 Take 225 g/8 oz gelatin icing. Mould the tea set — cups, saucers, teapot, sugar bowl and spoon, milk jug, knife and plates. A cocktail stick is a useful tool for making the smaller pieces.

6 To make the plates, cut out circles of icing with the small pastry cutter. Give the plates a scalloped edge with the cocktail stick before leaving them to dry. Leave each circle to dry in the bottom of a wine glass, which will form a lip around the edge of the plate. Mould the large cakes, small cakes and sandwiches.

7 Decorate the tea set with a fine paintbrush in a blue design. It can be simpler than the one illustrated. Leave to dry.

8 Take 450 g/1 lb fondant icing and colour deep yellow. Mould the separate sections of each bear — body, legs, arms, head, nose and ears — and leave to dry.

9 Assemble the three bears with small dabs of royal icing. With a darker yellow, paint in detail of their eyes, mouth, paws and body.

10 Take 125 g/4 oz gelatin icing. Make the stereo head set. Attach the headphones to the bear's head. Paint on the wires using black food colour. Paint the stereo black and silver and place it against the side of the bear.

11 Mould small squares from the remaining gelatin icing, fix the napkins in position and leave to dry. Paint each napkin with a bright check design. Assemble the cake.

EASTER CAKE

This pale yellow iced Easter cake is decorated around the sides and bottom border with piped grass, ducks, rabbits and flowers. In this instance these decorations are made with royal icing, but they could also be made with buttercream, chocolate or praline.

INGREDIENTS
1 × 20 cm/8 in round fruit cake
900 g/2 lb marzipan
900 g/2 lb royal icing
450 g/1 lb royal icing for piping

MATERIALS & DECORATIONS
1 × 25 cm/10 in round cake board
piping bag tip
nozzles
dessicated coconut
marzipan duck
Easter eggs
template
Food colours: green, yellow, orange, chocolate

1 Pipe around the bottom border of the cake with green royal icing.

2 Using the piping bag tip, pipe the bullrush leaves on the side of the cake with light green icing. Then pipe the bullrush heads with chocolate icing.

3 Embroider the small flowers on to the side of the cake with yellow icing.

4 Pipe a large shell border along the top edge of the cake. Leave to dry. Then overpipe a diagonal line across each shell with yellow icing. In turn, highlight the overpiped line with delicate green dots. This gives the finished cake a fresh and wholesome feeling of springtime.

5 To create the grass effect on top of the cake, spread a small quantity of royal icing in a thin layer across the centre, and before it dries, sprinkle some green coloured dessicated coconut over the royal icing.

6 Pipe the ducks on the side of the cake. Push out a teardrop shape, curled up at the end. Then pipe a dot for the head, and a small bead for the wing on the side. Using a fine nozzle, pipe the duck's beak and foot with orange icing.

7 The rabbit is piped on the side of the cake with a view of the rabbit's back. First pipe the rabbit's ears with long teardrops, then pipe a bead for the head, and a larger one for the body. Finally pipe a little white tail on the back of the rabbit.

8 To complete the cake, position marzipan ducks and a basket of eggs on the top.

CHRISTMAS PUDDING CAKE

The basis for this unusual Christmas cake is a spherical fruit cake. A spherical cake can also be decorated in other ways, for example as a football or tennis ball, or as a fruit.

INGREDIENTS
1 × 900 g/2 lb spherical fruit cake
450 g/1 lb marzipan
700 g/1½ lb fondant icing
175 g/6 oz royal icing for flooding

MATERIALS & DECORATIONS
1 × 23 cm/9 in round cake board
turntable (optional)
modelling tool
fine paintbrush (or edible pens)
sprig real or artificial holly
Food colours: brown, red, green

1 Use a 900 g/2 lb spherical tin without paper lining to bake this cake. Make sure the tin is well greased and floured. If used for baking as a sphere, the tin should have a small hole in the top to allow the steam to escape when cooked. Take the cake out of the tin while it is still hot — if you allow it to cool, the fats in the cake and around the tin will solidify, and it will be difficult to remove without spoiling its shape.

2 Drape the cake with marzipan, finishing it off neatly underneath. Leave the marzipan to dry for several hours. Then drape it with fondant icing, coloured deep brown.

3 To make the plate, cover a round 23 cm/9 in cake board with white fondant icing. Put it on the turntable and make the grooves with a knife or modelling tool.

4 A shaped tool makes an interesting moulded edge. It is much easier to do this kind of decoration on a turntable.

5 Paint a pattern on the edge of the plate to complete the effect, using the fine paintbrush and red and green food colours or red and green edible pens.

6 When you have completed the moulding, load the paintbrush with red food colour or use a red edible pen. Position the brush or pen for the red ring on the plate, hold it there and spin the turntable slowly until the ring is completed.

7 Place the cake on the plate and pour a small quantity of thick flooding icing over the top of the cake to create the effect of white sauce. Decorate the top with a sprig of real or artificial holly.

INDEX